Egypt's Pharaohs and Mummies Ancient History for Kids

Children's Ancient History

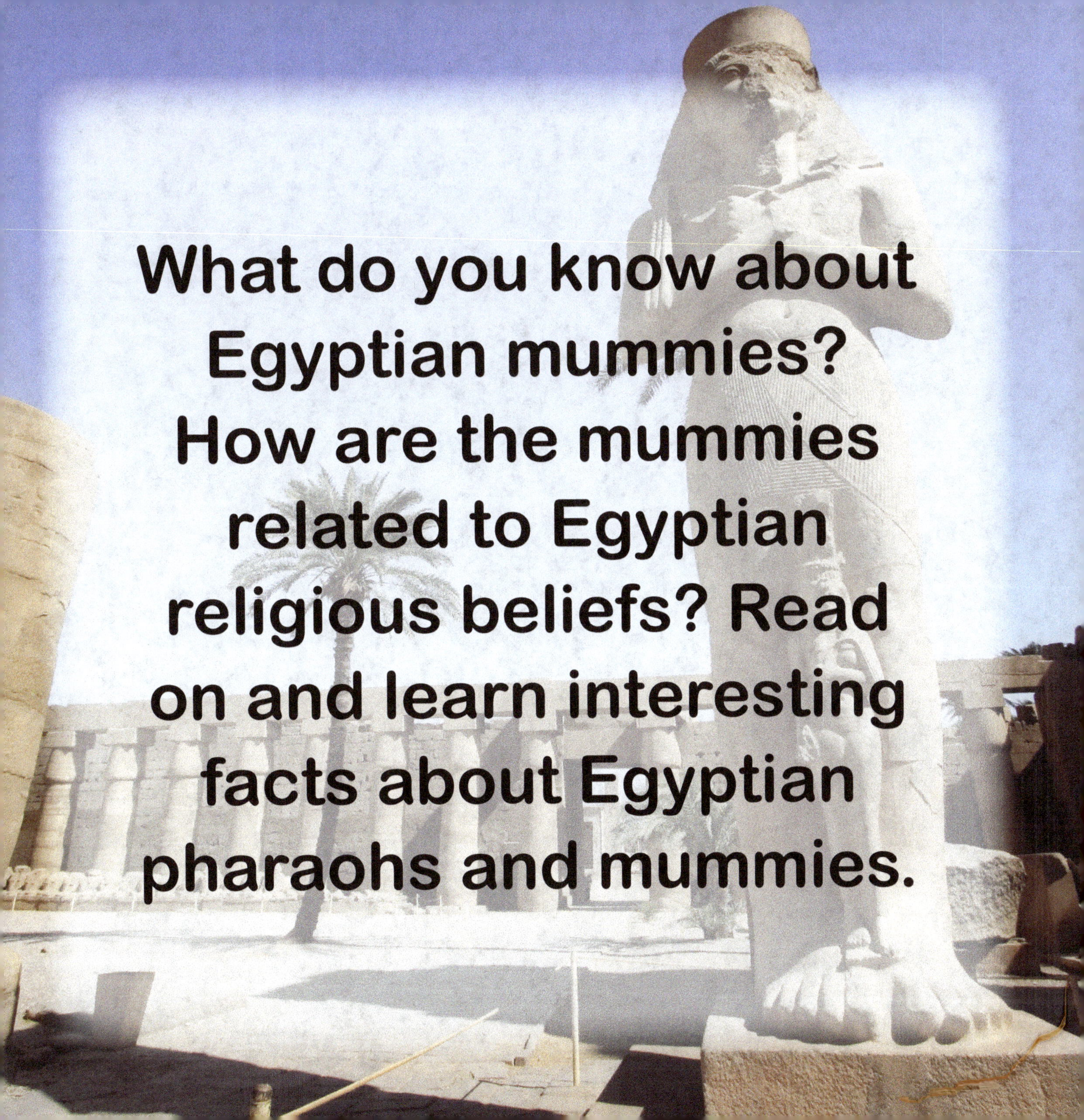

What do you know about Egyptian mummies? How are the mummies related to Egyptian religious beliefs? Read on and learn interesting facts about Egyptian pharaohs and mummies.

Who were the pharaohs? Pharaohs were the most powerful persons in the Egyptian kingdom. They were very important to Egypt. They owned all of Egypt. They were Egyptian kings and queens. Most pharaohs were men. However, Nefertiti and Cleopatra were two very popular pharaohs who were women.

A pharaoh was the head of the government in ancient Egypt. Every temple in ancient Egypt had the pharaoh as the high priest. A pharaoh was so powerful that Egyptians considered them as half-man and half-god.

Ancient Egyptians assumed that their pharaoh was the god Horus. He was the son of the sun god, Re. People believed that when their pharaoh died he would be united with the sun.

In ancient Egypt, the pharaoh was the political and religious leader of the people of Egypt. He was known as the "Lord of the Two Lands" and "the High Priest of Every Temple".

Kings were known as the early monarchs of Egypt. Members of the court called the kings as "your majesty" while rulers from other countries called them as "brothers". The title pharaoh started to be used during the New Kingdom, to refer to the king. The word pharaoh came to be no earlier than 1570 BCE. The most famous pharaoh of Egypt was Tutankhamun.

It it interesting to know
that the Egyptians
themselves did not call
their kings pharaohs. The
word Pharaoh is from
the Greek language. The
Greeks and Hebrews
used the word "pharaoh"
when they referred to
the Egyptian King.

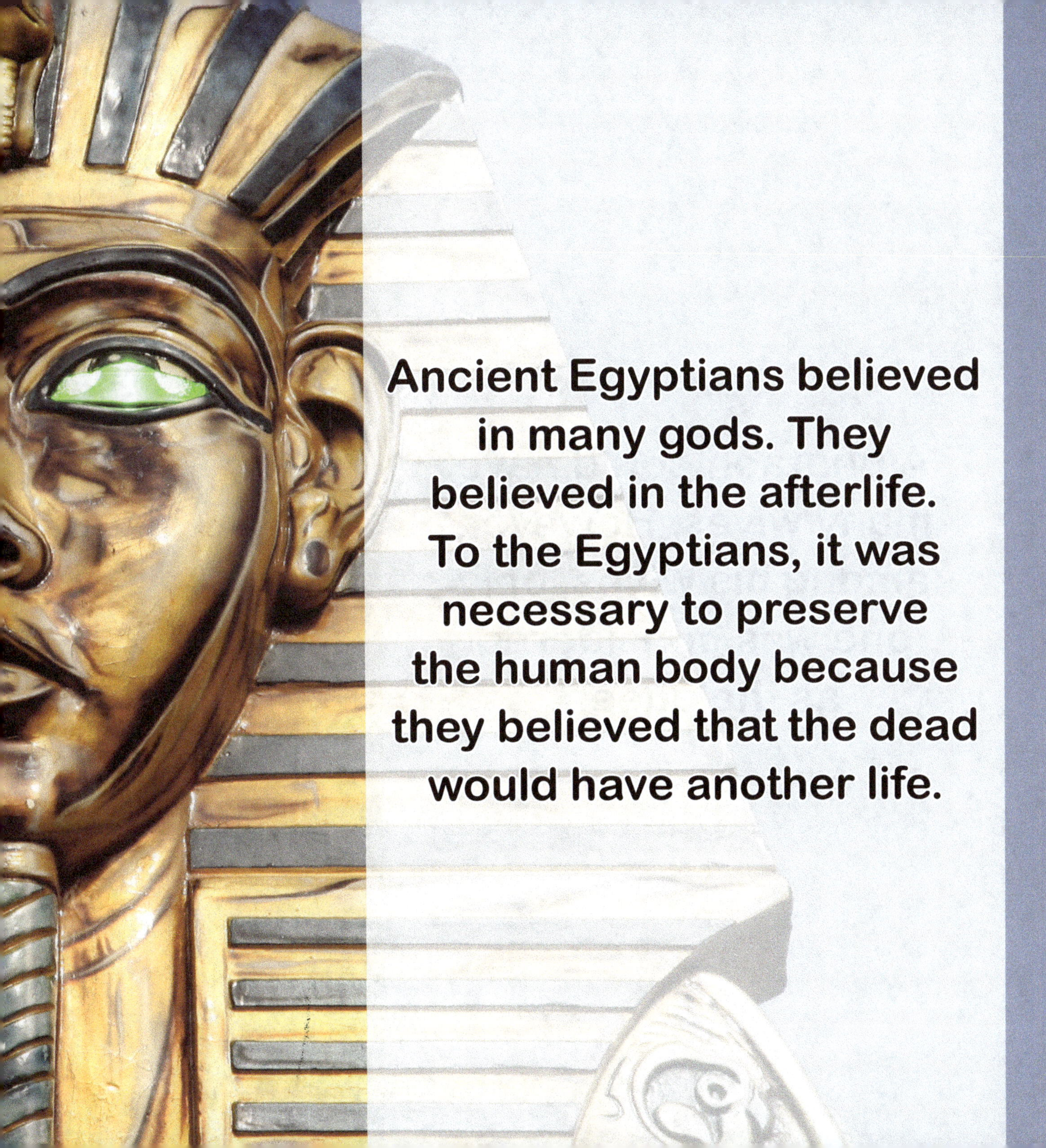

Ancient Egyptians believed in many gods. They believed in the afterlife. To the Egyptians, it was necessary to preserve the human body because they believed that the dead would have another life.

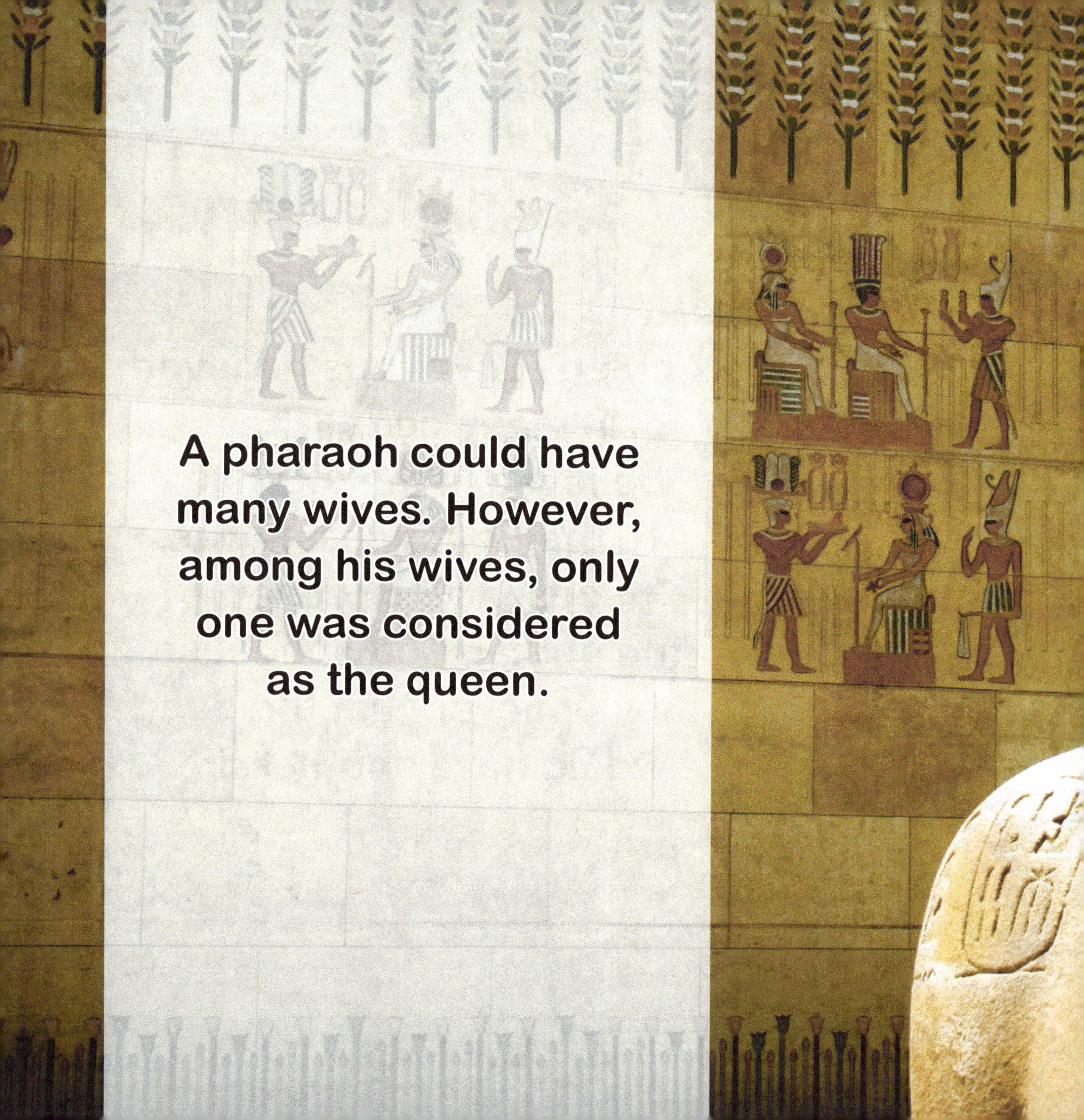

A pharaoh could have many wives. However, among his wives, only one was considered as the queen.

Pharaoh Pepi II became the King of Egypt when he was only 6 years old. He had the longest reign in history. He ruled Egypt from 2246 to 2152 BC: 86 years!

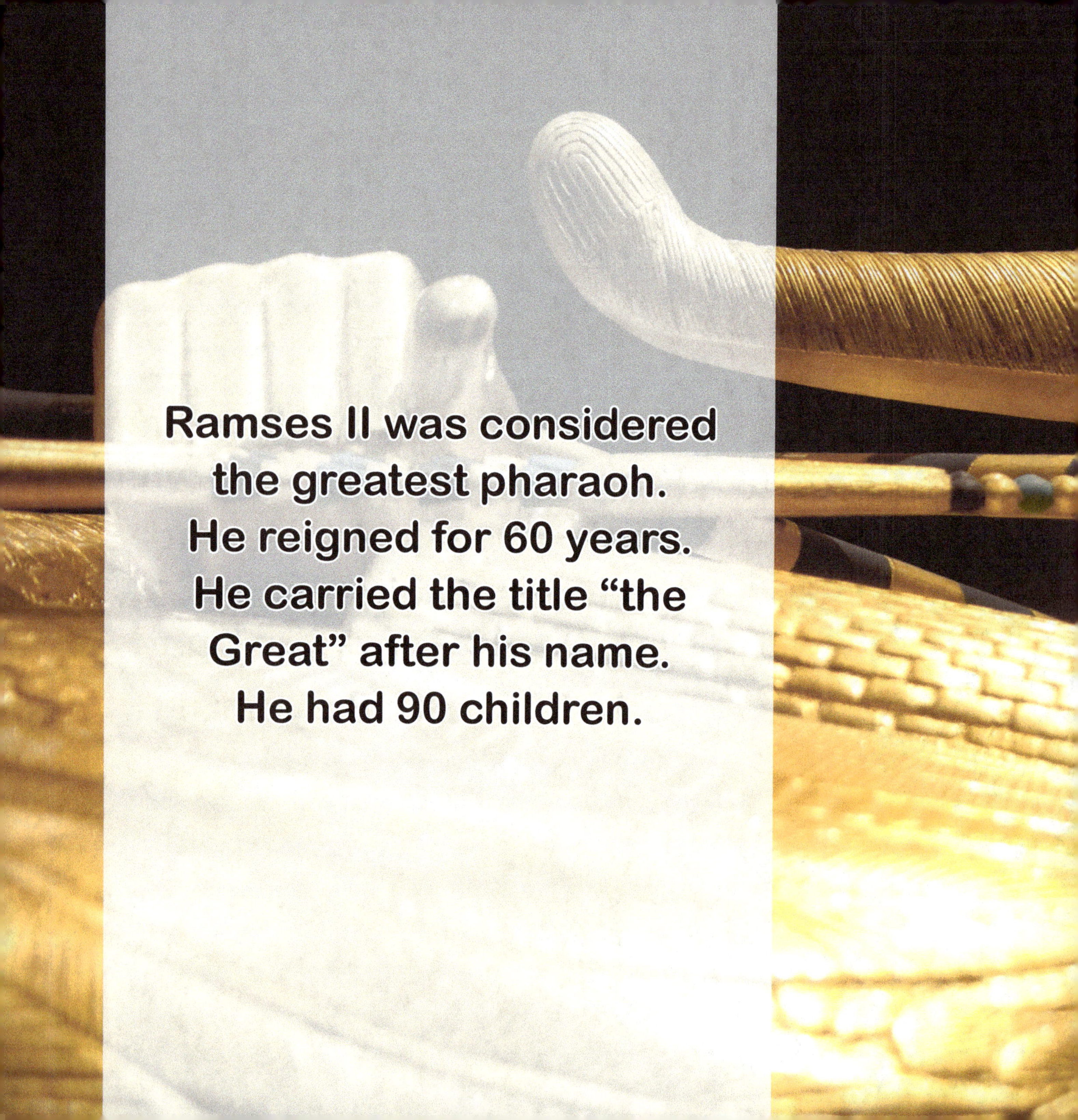
Ramses II was considered
the greatest pharaoh.
He reigned for 60 years.
He carried the title "the
Great" after his name.
He had 90 children.

It was the responsibility
of the pharaoh to keep
universal harmony in
Egypt. It was known as
"Ma'at". The pharaoh
was to defend his people
and his country.

Where were the Pharaohs buried? During the times of the Old and Middle Kingdoms of Egypt, kings were buried in pyramids. These pyramids were located on the edge of the desert.

One burial area was situated west of the ancient capital of Memphis. The Egyptians built pyramids for their dead pharaohs to house their bodies. They believed that if the pharaoh's body was mummified, the pharaoh would live forever.

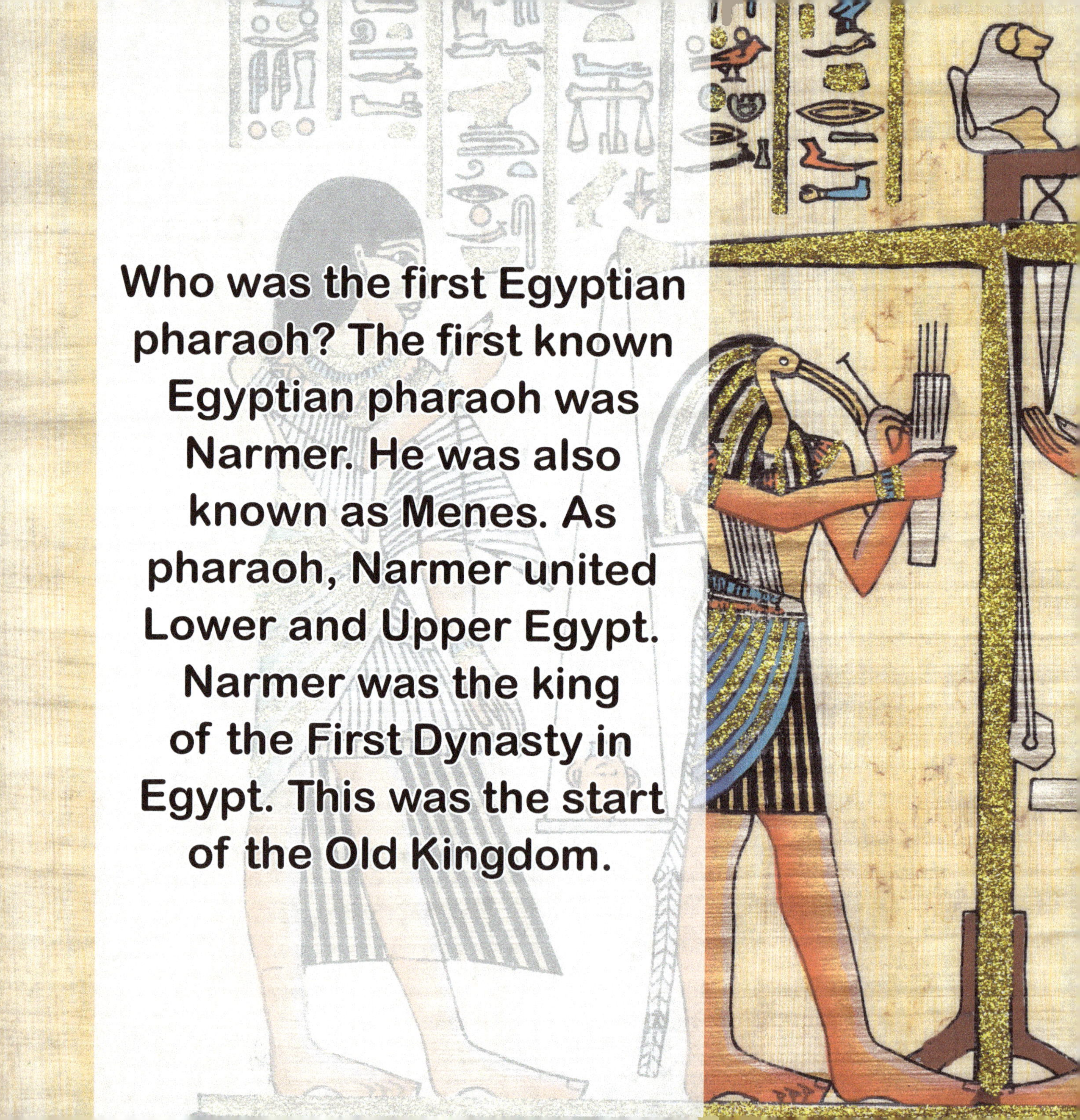

Who was the first Egyptian pharaoh? The first known Egyptian pharaoh was Narmer. He was also known as Menes. As pharaoh, Narmer united Lower and Upper Egypt. Narmer was the king of the First Dynasty in Egypt. This was the start of the Old Kingdom.

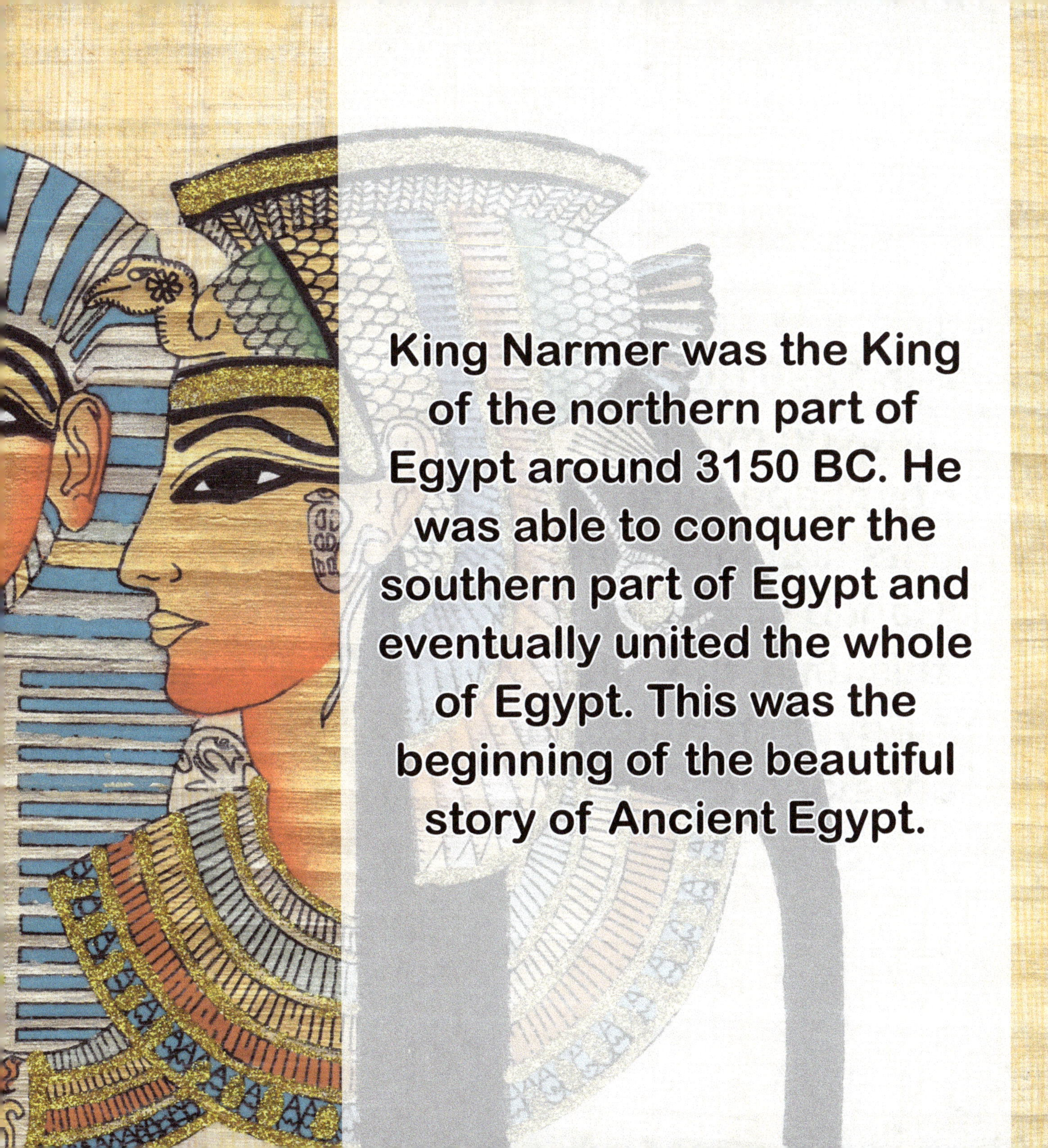

King Narmer was the King of the northern part of Egypt around 3150 BC. He was able to conquer the southern part of Egypt and eventually united the whole of Egypt. This was the beginning of the beautiful story of Ancient Egypt.

In 2890 BCE, the
second dynasty of
Egypt appeared and
its first king was
Raneb or Nebra. At
this time, the rulers
of Egypt started to be
considered as gods.

The mummification of a pharaoh was expensive. For the supreme ruler in Egypt, the mummification would include many gems and amulets.

The pharaohs' mummies were to be buried in a special burial place with all the expensive material possessions they had which were believed to be used in the afterlife.

King Narmer founded
the first capital of
Egypt, which was called
Memphis. The second
capital was Thebes.

What is the afterlife?
Ancient Egyptians
believed that when they
died they would make a
journey to another world.
They would live a new
life. Moreover, they had
to provide all the things
they thought the dead
needed in another life.

They would put all those things to the person's grave. However, poor Egyptians would just bury their dead in the sand.

They believed that
for the dead to lead a
new life, his body had
to be preserved. The
preserved body had
to be buried with all of
the possessions so that
he could use it to his
journey into the afterlife.

What is mummification?
It is the process used by
the Egyptians to preserve
their bodies after death.
It would take several days
to finish mummifying
a body. Organs were
removed except the
heart, for they believed
that it was the center of
intelligence and emotion.

The body was washed
and purified and filled
with stuffing. After
doing all the procedures
of mummification,
the body was placed
in a sarcophagus.

It was a stone coffin. After mummification, the ancient Egyptians believed that the mummy was ready for its journey in the afterlife.

The god of mummification was Anubis. He had the head of a jackal over his human body. That is why the priest who would be assigned to the burial would wear the mask of a jackal. It represented the god Anubis.

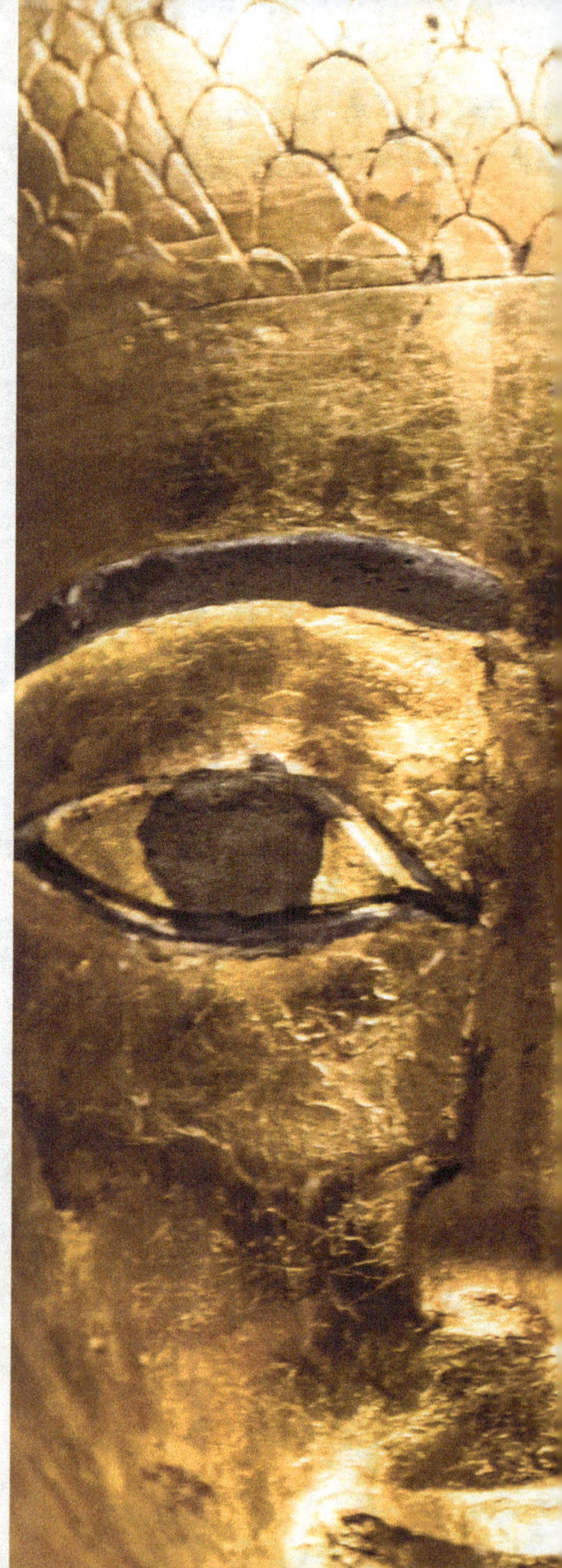

What are mummies?

For over 3,000 years,
ancient Egypt enjoyed
a successful society.
In hopes of preserving
human bodies, the
Egyptian priests
were able to develop
ways to mummify
the dead. Mummies
were the preserved
bodies of the dead.

In ancient Egypt, not only human bodies were preserved but also animals. Archaeologists have discovered discover burial chambers with mummified cats and other animals. Ancient Egyptians had cats as their most loved pets.

The story of Egypt has had an impact over the world. It's good to know the amazing stories of pharaohs, pyramids, and mummies. These among many fascinating features of Egyptian culture and history.

Visit

BABY PROFESSOR
EDUCATION KIDS

www.BabyProfessorBooks.com
to download Free Baby Professor eBooks
and view our catalog of new and exciting
Children's Books

www.ingramcontent.com/pod-product-compliance
Lightning Source LLC
Chambersburg PA
CBHW081230130726
47997CB00009B/2833